Alluring the Depths

Of

Taking

A

Risk

By

Robert gildon

Copyright © by (Robert Gildon 2023). All rights reserved. Before this document is duplicated or reproduced in any manner, the publisher's consent must be gained. Therefore, the contents within can neither be stored electronically, transferred, nor kept in a database. Neither in Part nor full can the document be copied, scanned, faxed, or retained without approval from the publisher or creator.

TABLE OF CONTENTS

Introduction......5
Chapter 1......14
The Evolution of Risk-Taking......14
*From Natural Adaptations to Strategic risk..14
*Risk as a Force for Human Advancement......27
Chapter 2......33
The Psychology of Risk......33
*Nature vs. Nurture and the risk-takers Mind.33
Chapter 3......40
Balancing Stability and Progress......40
*Risk as a Catalyst for Growth and Innovation...40
*The dark Aspect of Risk: Social and Economic Repercussions......46
Chapter 4......51
Mavericks and Gamblers: Famous Risk-Takers..51
*Revolution of the Mavericks & Visionaries...51
*Legends of Great Risk-Takers......55
Chapter 5......65
Beyond the Comfort Zone......65
*Dream-Chaser: The Pursuit Journey of Passion

65

*Getting Past Fear and Fighting Paralysis...... 76

Chapter 6.. 82

The Ethics of Risk: Balancing Responsibility and Ambition...82

*The Ethical Challenges of Taking Risks........ 82

*Leading ethically while navigating risks with honesty... 90

Chapter 7..97

Sports and the Pursuit of Glory......................98

*Pushing the Limits in Extreme Sports...........98

Chapter 8..113

Societal Impact of Risk................................. 114

*Political, medical, and social risks are intertwined...114

*Risks from Climate Change Worldwide....... 121

Chapter 9..127

Learning from Failure.................................. 128

*Lessons from Risk Gone Wrong: The Wisdom of Mistakes.. 128

*The Bottom Line: Embracing the Depths of Risk..132

Introduction

The concept of the allure of risk refers to the attraction or pull that people may experience when engaging in risky activities or seizing risky opportunities. It implies that taking risks has intrinsic appeal or excitement, despite the possibility of unfavorable results or repercussions, Taking chances can fundamentally alter you. You become bolder, stronger, and more self-assured as a result. They demonstrate your ability to decide, commit, and build the life you want. You develop confidence in yourself by realizing that you have succeeded in the past and can do so again. Even if things don't turn out precisely as you intended, taking a risk can be thrilling. "We don't manage risks so we can have no risk. We manage risks so that we can identify the ones that are worthwhile and will help us achieve our objectives. A rush of adrenaline and a sense of excitement are frequently produced by risky activities. Some people may find the thrill of uncertainty and the possibility of a positive outcome to be immensely stimulating and alluring. It is crucial to remember that while taking risks might result in positive outcomes, they also carry inherent risks and potential negative effects. Responsible decision-making requires evaluating risks, making educated choices, and taking potential outcomes into account. Each person has a different level of risk tolerance, therefore before engaging in any risky conduct or chasing risky chances, they must carefully assess the temptation of risk against the potential drawbacks.

Any deliberately or unconsciously managed behavior featuring a perceived lack of control over its result, as well as its potential advantages or disadvantages for one's own or others' physical, financial, or psychosocial well-being, is referred to as taking a risk. Risk-taking might be viewed as a test or as a chance to accomplish something worthwhile.

A strong motivation might be the prospect of conquering challenges, pushing one's limits, and achieving against the odds.

Risk is often allured by the possibility of large rewards.

The chance of reaching desired results can be alluring enough to overcome the perceived risks, *whether those outcomes are monetary rewards, personal development, or extraordinary experiences.* Because they do not set boundaries for themselves and are prepared to put up their best effort when everyone else is hesitating, courageous individuals are more likely to be successful.

Those who take measured risks are likely to be more intelligent than the typical person.

Taking risks can provide you with a break from your routine or monotony. *Theodore Roosevelt*, one of my most notable politicians, wrote beautifully about taking chances. If you fail, he claimed, at least you did so "while daring greatly." You won't ever experience success or failure if you don't take a risk. Some people may have a predisposition to take risks due to specific personality qualities, such as a high sensation-seeking threshold or a need for excitement.

These psychological elements may play a role in the appeal of risk as people look for new and challenging experiences. In actuality, taking risks is a necessary component of proper growth. Risks are frequently viewed by people as being intrinsically bad. This can't be. Risks are decisions with ambiguous possible results that may or may not be desirable. Risky activity can occasionally be connected to prestige, acclaim, or social admiration.

People could be persuaded to take risks by the perceived status or reputation that goes along with it, particularly in fields like extreme sports, business, or risky activities.

Although taking risks is frequently viewed as something to be worried about, when done well, they can yield wonderful rewards. Risk-taking is crucial for business owners who wish to succeed. It necessitates going beyond what one would normally do in terms of pushing their limits; we all know thousands of people who have impulsive or overly cautious tendencies yet nonetheless perform exceptionally well in their careers. We must all encounter risk in our life since it implies taking a chance, trying a fresh approach, and possibly failing or succeeding. One of the most important methods to develop one's abilities and gain experience is to take risks.

Chapter 1

The Evolution of Risk-Taking

*From Natural Adaptations to Strategic risk

Risk-taking has a long history in the history of the human race, and it has been crucial to the development of civilizations. Our collective path has been shaped by brave people who took calculated risks, from ancient explorers setting out on perilous expeditions to modern entrepreneurs pushing the envelope.

Risk-taking has always been a necessary component of humanity's ambition for exploration and growth.

The instinctive need to survive has been firmly imprinted in our DNA throughout history. The ability of our species to adapt, invent, and flourish in the face of difficulty is a core trait that has carried us ahead. But just as society has developed, so have our means of survival.

The human path has been one of astonishing metamorphosis, from the rudimentary instincts that helped our ancestors negotiate dangerous surroundings to the calculated risks that influence our decisions today. Our ancestors were guided by their survival instincts in the early phases of human evolution as they navigated a world filled with dangers. Finding food, looking for shelter, and defending oneself from predators were all part of these instincts' core repertoire. Survival instincts evolved into collective ones over time as groups grew and information was disseminated. This led to cooperation, communication, and the emergence of primitive social structures.

The advancement of our species was made possible by this attitude of cooperation. The risk was largely avoided since it was thought to pose a threat to survival. But this fear of taking chances prevented us from venturing into unexplored territory and slowed down our development.

A significant change happened at a specific time in our history. People started to understand that taking prudent risks may yield huge returns. Individuals accepted uncertainty as a chance for growth rather than giving in to a dread of the unknown.

Scientific breakthroughs, commercial ventures, and societal progress were all the result of calculated bets.

This change signaled a turning point in human history and pushed us toward previously unimaginable accomplishments. **The Space Race**, an unparalleled rivalry, took place in the middle of the **20th century**. To capture the last frontier, the **Soviet Union and the United States** set out on a risky adventure.

Why do we deliberately incur risks? Our capacity to evaluate probability, consider possible outcomes, and balance potential advantages and losses is what distinguishes us from other people. A fine line must be drawn between intuition and reason to successfully navigate this complex decision-making process. A thorough understanding of risk management, resilience, and adaptation is necessary for the art of taking measured risks, whether one is a scientist exploring a ground-breaking concept or an entrepreneur investing in a new enterprise.

The explorers of the Age of Discovery, like Ferdinand Magellan, risked everything by venturing into the unknown. Their boldness changed not just the physical boundaries of the world but also the collective human psyche. We continue to be defined by our curiosity, adaptability, and resilience, which were cultivated by the spirit of exploration. Social movements throughout history have been fueled by risk-taking in the pursuit of justice and equality. People have boldly confronted unjust systems, risking their lives and livelihoods for a more equitable society, from the abolition of slavery and suffrage movements to the civil rights and LGBTQ+ rights movements. *These social risks have had a lasting influence on our collective consciousness through reshaping societies, tearing down discriminatory institutions, and fostering tolerance.*

The world of business and entrepreneurship depends on taking calculated risks. Entrepreneurs with a clear vision, such as **Thomas Edison**, **Henry Ford**, and **Steve Jobs,** had the guts to go after disruptive ideas and alter entire sectors. They opened doors for economic development, technical innovation, and employment creation by questioning the current quo. These risk-takers have advanced civilization by revolutionizing the way we live, work, and interact. They were armed with tenacity and an unyielding faith in their ideas. Taking risks frequently requires overcoming challenges and setbacks.

Our collective resiliency has been formed by the lessons we've earned from historical people who overcame difficult odds.

The courage of people like **Malala Yousafzai and Nelson Mandela**, as well as **Winston Churchill's** unshakable leadership during World War II, and their tenacity in the face of adversity are examples of people whose tales encourage us to take on difficulties head-on and endure.

They have demonstrated to us the transformative power of resilience via their courage and tenacity. **Scientists like Galileo Galilei and Isaac Newton** risked persecution in the 17th *century* to question accepted doctrine to solve the universe's mysteries.

Their revolutionary findings not only revolutionized our understanding of physics and astronomy but also sparked a paradigm change in how people think. We discover the tremendous significance of their intellectual fearlessness and how it set the route for scientific advancement by examining the inherent hazards they faced. Rapid technical developments were brought about by the Industrial Revolution, which changed cultures and economics.

To harness the force of electricity, visionaries like **Thomas Edison and Nikola Tesla** took big risks, while businessmen like **Andrew Carnegie and John D.** Numerous examples of calculated risks that have changed society can be found throughout history. These people dared to confront the current quo and accept uncertainty, from **Christopher Columbus'** exploratory expeditions to **Marie Curie's** scientific discoveries. Examples from today's field of technology can be seen in the innovative endeavors of entrepreneurs like **Elon Musk and Jeff Bezos,** who are pushing the bounds of what is conceivable. Human development has been nothing short of amazing, spanning from our innate survival instincts to the calculated risks that propel advancement today.

As a species, we have advanced thanks to our capacity for adaptability, planning, and taking calculated risks. Our capacity to handle risks becomes crucial in the face of previously unheard-of global concerns like pandemics and climate change. Risk-taking has been a fundamental driver of human progress throughout history, it becomes obvious as we consider the tapestry of human history. Taking chances has pushed us forward, thanks to the boldness of explorers, the ingenuity of scientists, and the tenacity of modern businesses.

*Risk as a Force for Human Advancement

Risk is frequently seen as a bad thing since it is connected to danger and uncertainty. But as we dig further, we find that risk is an essential component of what propels human development.

Great advances and accomplishments have been made throughout history by people and communities that were ready to take calculated risks. Risk-taking is essential to innovation. People and organizations can make ground-breaking discoveries and advances when they dare to question the status quo and go out into uncharted waters. Many of the most revolutionary discoveries in history from technological wonders to scientific breakthroughs were the result of calculated risks.

Risk and exploration are inextricably linked. Insatiable curiosity and a willingness to take on unknowable risks have propelled brave explorers throughout history to set out on risky treks over uncharted oceans, impenetrable jungles, and enormous deserts. These adventurers increased our knowledge of the world, uncovered uncharted territory, and built trade routes, promoting cross-cultural interaction and socioeconomic advancement.

They set the groundwork for globalization and the interconnected world we live in today via their daring and quest for knowledge. Individual risk-taking is not just seen in the fields of invention and exploration. It also includes developing personally and finding oneself.

Deep personal growth can result from stepping outside of our comfort zones, accepting new challenges, and embracing uncertainty. Each risk we take offers an opportunity to learn, adapt, and grow, whether it's taking on a new professional path, starting a business, or even participating in risky activities.

We discover latent potential and enhance resilience, inventiveness, and adaptability by overcoming challenges and pushing our boundaries. Although taking risks is necessary for success, it must be combined with careful risk management. Assessing potential outcomes, comprehending probability, and putting mitigation plans into practice are all parts of calculated risk-taking.

We may use risk as a growth engine by striking a balance between ambition and caution. Risk naturally elicits fear in us because it exposes us to the unknown and the possibility of failure. To fully leverage the power of risk, though, we must learn to get past this anxiety and develop an attitude that welcomes uncertainty. To enable people to take calculated risks, it is essential to promote education, a supportive environment, and a culture that values creativity and resiliency. We can encourage a new generation of risk-takers who will define the future by redefining risk as an opportunity rather than a danger.

Chapter 2
The Psychology of Risk

*Nature vs. Nurture and the risk-takers Mind

Psychologists and scholars have been interested in the human ability for risk-taking behavior for decades. Some people appear to be natural risk-takers, whereas others approach life cautiously and dislike the unknown. The relative importance of nature (genetics) versus nurture (environment and upbringing) in determining risk-taking behavior has been the subject of a long-running controversy. The nature defense contends that a person's genetic makeup has a role in determining their propensity for taking risks.

According to research, some genes are linked to a higher predisposition for risk-taking behavior. Examples of genetic variants that affect how someone reacts to rewarding and unpleasant stimuli include those related to dopamine receptors, serotonin transporters, and neuropeptide systems. *These genetic characteristics may have an impact on a person's impulsivity, sensation-seeking instincts, and tolerance for ambiguity,* all of which play a role in risk-taking tendencies. While nature supplies the genetic blueprint, it is important to recognize that nurture also plays a significant part in influencing the risk-takers mindset.

The environment has a major impact on whether risk-taking inclinations are encouraged or discouraged. An individual's propensity for taking risks can be influenced by a variety of factors, including upbringing, family dynamics, socioeconomic status, cultural influences, and exposure to risk-taking role models. For instance, growing up in a setting that values calculated risk-taking, and promotes discovery, and rewards can have a big impact on a person's propensity to take chances later in life.

It is critical to comprehend how nature and nurture interact in complicated ways to shape the risk-takers mentality rather than seeing them as distinct forces. Risk-taking tendencies can increase or decrease depending on how heredity and the environment interact. When there are possibilities for taking risks and earning rewards as a result, genetic predispositions may be more likely to appear. Similarly, the impact on the environment may reduce or increase a natural propensity for taking risks.

Understanding this complex dynamic can offer important insights into how risk-taking behavior develops. Beyond the question of nature vs. nurture, a risk-taking mindset is also influenced by personality traits and cognitive factors. *Some people are more likely to take risks because they have a natural tendency for sensation-seeking, novelty-seeking, or a high tolerance for uncertainty.*

In addition, cognitive traits like decision-making, self-perception, and the capacity to weigh risks and rewards are crucial in defining a person's propensity for taking risks. These elements influence the general risk-takers mindset by interacting with both nature and nurture.

Understanding the interaction between nature and nurture offers important insights for people trying to develop a risk-taking mindset.

While genetics serve as a foundation, the environment and individual experiences provide a wealth of options for development. People can cultivate and hone their risk-taking abilities by purposefully exposing themselves to novel situations, accepting calculated risks, and building resilience in the face of uncertainty. The risk-taker mindset can be strengthened further by developing self-awareness, developing decision-making skills, and looking for mentors and role models.

Chapter 3
Balancing Stability and Progress

*Risk as a Catalyst for Growth and Innovation

Businesses and people alike face countless dangers in a world that is changing quickly and where change is the only constant. The risk may be a potent force for innovation and progress, even though it is frequently linked to unpredictability and bad results. Risk is fundamentally the likelihood that a bad thing will happen. It includes a wide range of elements, including competitive dynamics, market volatility, and technology upheavals. Risk is a necessary component of any company environment, despite the difficulties and possible hazards it can provide. Organizations must embrace a mindset that reframes risk as an opportunity for transformation and progress rather than avoiding it. Any successful organization depends on innovation. Businesses may adopt, stand out from the competition, and add value for customers.

A key component of the innovation process is risk. Organizations may build an environment that promotes experimentation, innovation, and the pursuit of game-changing ideas by challenging accepted norms and accepting ambiguity. True innovation cannot exist without risk. Risk-taking is a trait that distinguishes entrepreneurs. They understand that taking calculated risks is essential to upending markets, launching new products, and stimulating the economy. Successful business people are aware that failure is simply a stepping stone on the road to success rather than the end. Entrepreneurs continuously push the envelope and venture into uncharted territory by taking calculated risks, which results in game-changing breakthroughs that reshape whole sectors. Organizations must promote a risk-tolerant culture if they want to use risk as a driver of innovation and growth. To accomplish this, an environment must be created where staff members feel free to take measured chances and learn from both successes and failures. Such a culture must prioritize open communication, promote original thought, and provide opportunities for experimentation. Innovative ideas are more likely to be produced when teams and individuals feel encouraged to pursue innovation. Risk is necessary for growth, but it must be managed and its potential negative effects must be reduced.

Organizations must create solid risk management plans that include recognizing, evaluating, and tracking risks. Businesses can take proactive steps to overcome obstacles and use data-driven insights to make decisions that are well-informed and less likely to result in significant setbacks. Organizations that practice effective risk management are more likely to balance innovation with stability. This section offers a few noteworthy case studies to demonstrate how risk can act as a driver for innovation and progress. It looks at businesses that took on risk, profited from uncertainty, and made important strides in their respective fields.

These true tales motivate by demonstrating how taking calculated risks can result in amazing results.

*The dark Aspect of Risk: Social and Economic Repercussions

Risk is an ever-present companion that affects all areas of our lives in our fast-changing environment. While risk is frequently seen as a vital component of development and innovation, it also has a negative aspect. Our risk-related decisions can have a significant impact on society as a whole. The delicate balance between taking risks and societal well-being is examined in this section. It looks at case studies where excessive risk-taking or a lack of risk management strategies had serious social repercussions. *We examine the cascading consequences that can affect communities and people, ranging from environmental catastrophes to financial crashes.* The economy and risk are inextricably linked. The hidden economic consequences of risk are examined in this section. It explores how unmanaged risk harms businesses, sectors, and the overall stability of economies. Case studies of financial institution failures and stock market crashes serve as cautionary tales, emphasizing the negative effects of reckless risk-taking on the economy over the long term. Uneven risk distribution frequently makes already existing social inequities worse. We investigate the significant societal ramifications that may result by examining the structural variables that contribute to this imbalance, *such as unequal access to resources and decision-making procedures.*

Risk harms people and societies psychologically in addition to its physical effects. It examines how stress, anxiety, and fear can infiltrate society and have an impact on people's mental health and general well-being. It also looks into the influence of risk perception on public opinion and policy choices. *Although the negative aspects of risk can be intimidating, this section offers encouragement by presenting techniques for prudent risk management.* Case studies on effective risk mitigation strategies offer light on doable strategies that help lessen the negative effects of risk.

Chapter 4

Mavericks and Gamblers: Famous Risk-Takers

*Revolution of the Mavericks & Visionaries

The mavericks and visionaries who dare to defy the status quo and take risks can change the world in a society that is frequently characterized by conformity and a fear of the unfamiliar. Mavericks and visionaries have an uncompromising zeal, unshakeable faith in their ideas, and the courage to forge through in the face of difficulty and failure.

They transform industries, ignite innovation, and inspire generations thanks to their audacity and tenacity. Visionaries and outliers aren't scared to challenge traditional wisdom and consider unorthodox concepts. They have a special capacity for looking beyond the bounds of convention and seeing a future that others might find inconceivable. They transform current systems, disrupt industries, and create new markets by questioning the established quo.

Failure is not a setback but rather a stepping stone to achievement for mavericks and visionaries. They accept the prospect of failure even if they are aware that taking risks presents a chance for development and learning. Mavericks and visionaries have the intrinsic ability to think up big, unconventional ideas. They have the guts to aggressively explore ideas that others deem inconceivable. Whether it was **Martin Luther King Jr.'s** revolutionary idea for civil rights or **Mark Zuckerberg's** bold ambition to connect the entire world through

Facebook, these people challenged social norms and sparked significant change. Mavericks and visionaries have disrupted entire industries through their risk-taking initiatives, changing how we live, work, and engage with the outside world.

Mavericks and visionaries leave a lasting mark on history with their deeds and accomplishments, motivating succeeding generations to dream large and take chances. Young people's imaginations are sparked by their stories, inspiring them to follow their passions and change the world. The spirit of innovation and advancement is embodied by mavericks and visionaries. They question social norms, alter industries, and inspire future generations because of their unwavering determination and willingness to take chances.

*Legends of Great Risk-Takers

Tales of Legendary Risk-Takers is a captivating collection of tales that honors those who dared to venture outside of their comfort zones and take advantage of the opportunities that life offered them. These exceptional people, who range from business owners and explorers to artists and visionaries, personify the traits of fearlessness and resiliency and serve as a constant reminder that tremendous rewards frequently await those who are willing to take calculated risks. entrepreneurs who went against the grain and created their success by following their paths. We learn priceless lessons from these successful business people that might encourage budding entrepreneurs to take calculated risks and pursue their aspirations with unyielding tenacity, starting with **Steve Jobs'** bold development of Apple Inc. Join the fearless explorers who stretched the limits of human knowledge and widened the horizons of our understanding as they set off on an exhilarating journey. We see their unwavering pursuit of discovery, even in the face of overwhelming obstacles, from **Christopher Columbus'** fabled voyage to the New World to **Jacques Cousteau's** underwater odysseys. These adventurers serve as a reminder that curiosity may lead to unprecedented opportunities and change the course of history when it is paired with the courage to step into the unknown.

Explore the world of creative risk-takers who questioned established conventions and changed their respective areas. We honor the force of artistic expression, from **Vincent van Gogh's** daring brushstrokes that permanently changed the art world to **Bob Dylan's** musical lyrical revolt. Their experiences show us how accepting uncertainty and departing from the norm may result in ground-breaking artistic accomplishments that have a lasting impact on society's cultural fabric. We investigate the lives of these unsung heroines who bravely pursue their passions in professions that are predominantly male, from ***Ada Lovelace***, the first computer programmer in history, to ***Grace Hopper***, a pioneer of computer science. Their experiences serve as examples of the human soul's tenacious spirit and its capacity to overcome challenges, demonstrating that greatness may arise from the most unexpected places. There is a small group of successful people who have the extraordinary quality of boldness. These people venture forth on less-traveled pathways, reject conventional wisdom, and embrace uncertainty. They are trailblazers who take risks, question the status quo, and push the envelope of what is possible. Follow in **Amelia Earhart's** footsteps as she went to the skies, or climb Mount Everest's perilous slopes with **Sir Edmund Hillary** and **Tenzing Norgay.** These intrepid individuals motivate us to face uncertainty head-on and unlock our amazing potential.

Find out the tales of intrepid businessmen and entrepreneurs who upended conventional wisdom and changed entire industries. Learn about **Oprah Winfrey's** audacity to change media and entertainment, as well as **Richard Branson's** courage in leading Virgin Group into unexplored territory. These rebels show that fortune does reward those who aren't afraid to question the existing quo. *Witness the outstanding achievements of* **Nikola Tesla,** *whose forward-thinking concepts helped create contemporary electrical systems, and* **Marie Curie,** *whose fearless pursuit of her radioactive studies permanently altered the face of science.* These humanitarians remind us that bravery can be a cause for significant positive change in the world, from **Mother Teresa's** persistent dedication to helping the poor and disenfranchised to **Malala Yousafzai's** gutsy battle for girls' education. From **Frida Kahlo** and **Vincent van Gogh** to **Pablo Picasso** and **David Bowie,** we see their tenacious pursuit of self-expression and their readiness to defy social standards.

Their creativity demonstrates how luck benefits those who courageously express their voices and rebel against the current system. Through their unyielding resolve and unshakeable belief in themselves, these icons from **Muhammad Ali's** refusal to give up to **Serena Williams'** unrelenting pursuit of victory pushed the bounds of human achievement.

Their experiences serve as a reminder that success favors those who are willing to work beyond their physical and mental capabilities to achieve it. We are motivated by their experiences to question the status quo, go after our goals, and face challenges head-on with unyielding resolve. The lives of these illustrious risk-takers serve as a reminder that individuals who have the guts to leave their comfort zones and leave a lasting impression on the world may find success. Let their tales inspire a glimmer of boldness in each of us.

Chapter 5
Beyond the Comfort Zone

*Dream-Chaser: The Pursuit Journey of Passion

The pursuit of one's ambitions is a strong force that propels people to venture outside of the norm and set out on risky journeys in life. To pursue your aspirations, you must be willing to take risks, venture into the unknown, and disregard social conventions. To succeed in this enthralling endeavor, people must muster up tremendous courage, tenacity, and a dogged drive to follow their passions. Dreams have a special appeal that draws our emotions and satisfies our wants. They act as a guiding light, pointing us in the direction of a destiny that is consistent with who we are. The idea of pursuing our aspirations energizes us and gives us a feeling of direction, allowing us to escape the routine of daily life. But it's important to understand that this goal requires sacrifices and presents us with uncertainty, so it's not for the weak of the heart. Exploring new areas is one of the qualities of chasing dreams. People must venture outside of their comfort zones and openly embrace the unknown. There are no assurances of success or set routes to take in this exhilarating endeavor. Instead, we must maneuver through uncertainty while taking calculated risks and failing wisely. We unlock latent skills that would have otherwise remained dormant by embracing the unknown and realizing our potential. Chasing dreams requires violating accepted standards and disobeying social rules. It frequently entails departing from conventional job pathways or societal expectations, arousing others' mistrust and distrust. *It takes tremendous courage and unwavering self-belief to overcome these external influences.* Dream-chasing is not without its share of challenges. Along the journey, obstacles like money restrictions, self-doubt, and failure anxiety can be extremely difficult.

But when faced with difficulty, our actual strength manifests itself. Every challenge becomes a chance for *development, resiliency, and self-discovery.* The capacity to adjust, persevere, and take lessons from failure ultimately helps us move closer to achieving our goals. Chasing dreams is a journey that transforms our character and shifts our viewpoints, not only about getting to a particular place. We learn priceless life lessons through this endeavor, including the value of tenacity, the requirement of self-belief, and the strength of resilience. These teachings go well beyond the domain of our aspirations, enabling us to take on difficulties in the future with unshakeable tenacity. In the process of achieving our goals, we inexorably redefine what success is. It goes beyond financial possessions or societal acceptance to express personal fulfillment and live following our passions. It is possible to develop a strong feeling of authenticity and purpose by having the confidence to pursue our aspirations, which results in a life that is more meaningful and fulfilling. Pursuing your dreams is fundamentally driven by the overwhelming urge of passion.

It is a force that compels people to look for fulfillment outside of the box. Passion stokes a fire inside, inspiring people to risk everything and make significant life choices. To follow your passion, you must venture outside of your comfort zone, face your fears, and accept that there will be dangers along the way. To pursue your aspirations, you must be open to the unknown. It involves taking risks, whether it's starting a business, pursuing a creative project, or making a significant change in one's job. Dream chasers expose themselves to uncertainty, instability, and the chance of failure by stepping outside of the familiar. Yet true innovation and personal development thrive in these undiscovered regions. Risk will always be present when pursuing your dreams. *It includes concerns about financial instability, cultural pressures, failure,* and making sacrifices for others. Dream chasers must confront these dangers with bravery, resiliency, and a firm trust in their skills. They are aware that setbacks and failures are not barriers to success, but rather stepping stones. *Each risk taken turns into a worthwhile lesson acquired, strengthening their resolve to keep going.* Fear is frequently the biggest obstacle to achieving dreams. The fear of failing, the fear of being judged, and the fear of the unknown may be crippling. Dream chasers learn their true power, though, when they face and accept these concerns. They develop a firm belief in their goal while learning to silence the voices of doubt. Their resilience and unshakable dedication to their dreams are demonstrated by their ability to overcome fear. Even while following your passion involves some risk, the benefits are enormous. Pursuing goals gives one a sense of direction, fulfillment, and a genuine connection to their inner self.

It enables people to reach their maximum potential, releasing their creativity and advancing society. Pursuing one's aspirations encourages self-improvement, resiliency, and unflinching faith in one's skills, transforming people into their best selves. Beyond bringing about personal fulfillment, following your aspirations motivates others to do the same. Dream chasers transform into inspirational role models who inspire others to follow their ambitions and follow their passions. They dismantle the social obstacles that keep others in mediocrity by exemplifying the willingness to take chances. Their trip serves as an example of how following one's heart can transform.

*Getting Past Fear and Fighting Paralysis

Fear is a strong feeling that frequently renders us helpless and keeps us from realizing our full potential. It has the power to prevent us from going after our goals, taking chances, and seizing fresh possibilities. However, by comprehending fear and discovering ways to conquer it, we can escape its hold and lead lives that are more important and rewarding. Humans naturally experience fear in the presence of perceived threats or risks. It sets off a variety of physiological and emotional responses intended to keep us secure. But in contemporary society, anxiety frequently takes on irrational or exaggerated forms that impede our ability to advance both personally and professionally.

Fear frequently leads to paralysis. It paralyzes us, keeping us from making choices, taking chances, or achieving our objectives. To actively work toward eliminating fear, we must first recognize when it is producing paralysis in our lives. Various facets of our lives can suffer as a result of fear and paralysis. They may restrict our ability to advance professionally, develop meaningful personal connections, and generally be happy. We become inspired to face and conquer fear and paralysis when we are aware of the harmful impacts that they can have. Recognizing your fear is the first step to getting over it. We might start to face our fears by acknowledging and accepting them. Limiting ideas and negative self-talk are frequent causes of fear. It takes work to get over your phobia. By stepping out of our comfort zone in modest, gradual steps, we may reach out to people who can offer advice and support during trying times. We can overcome our fears with their support.

Make a plan to reach your goals and clearly explain them. A sense of direction and purpose can assist prevent paralysis. Complex tasks frequently result in paralysis. To move forward and gather momentum, divide them into more manageable, smaller steps. Failure fear has the power to paralyze us. Reframe failure as a beneficial learning opportunity that fosters resilience and personal growth. Be kind to yourself and practice self-kindness.

Recognize that obstacles and problems are a necessary part of the trip, and permit yourself to grow as a result. It takes guts to fight immobility and face fear. It entails stepping beyond our comfort zones, accepting uncertainty, and acting despite our concerns. Our real potential can be unlocked and success in both our personal and professional lives can be attained by creating a mindset of courage and a practice of taking calculated risks. On the road to personal development and fulfillment, fear, and immobility can be strong roadblocks. We can, however, escape their hold if we comprehend fear, recognize paralysis, and put these concepts into practice. It is possible to live a life that is motivated by achievement, resilience, and purpose when we embrace bravery and take action.

Chapter 6

The Ethics of Risk: Balancing Responsibility and Ambition

*The Ethical Challenges of Taking Risks

Risk-taking is a natural element of being a human in the complex environment we live in today. People frequently face moral quandaries related to taking risks, whether they are starting a new business enterprise, going on a risky adventure, or making important decisions. Risks contain the potential for unpleasant events that test our moral compass, even while they can also result in positive outcomes and personal growth. Risk-taking refers to consciously making choices or undertaking actions that could have unfavorable repercussions.

These dangers, nevertheless, can also bring about great rewards and personal joy. The Risk-takers should think about the ethical ramifications of their decisions because they may affect not just their own lives but also the lives of others. The importance of striking a balance between societal obligations and personal goals increases. The common good and communal principles may clash with the pursuit of personal ambitions, though.

The moral conundrum emerges when the potential rewards of taking a risk for oneself come at the expense of others or go against accepted moral principles.

The utilitarian perspective emphasizes enhancing overall enjoyment and reducing harm while making ethical decisions. People must weigh the possible benefits of taking risks against the risks of unfavorable outcomes to gauge the overall impact. Risk-taking frequently has unforeseen consequences that can be detrimental to other people or society as a whole. *A huge moral dilemma arises when deciding whether the possible advantages exceed these unanticipated negative effects. Regardless of the results,* deontological approaches place a higher priority on upholding ethical obligations and principles. To ensure they uphold core ethical standards in the pursuit of goals, people must balance the risks inherent in their acts with the moral imperatives motivating those actions. The conflict between immediate benefits and long-term effects is another aspect of the moral quandaries associated with taking risks. Even though taking risks can have immediate benefits, doing so may also have long-term negative effects. Risks and benefits must be evaluated holistically in light of ethical issues to ensure that short-term gains do not come at the expense of long-term welfare. Virtue ethics place a strong emphasis on the formation of moral principles and values. Risk-takers should think about the values they exemplify, such as courage, honesty, and integrity, and make sure their behaviors are consistent with these virtues. Taking risks is frequently linked to exercising one's freedom and liberty. As long as they don't interfere with the rights and interests of others, people should be free to pursue their goals and assume the risks involved. In exchange for certain liberties, society expects people to behave responsibly and think about the interests of others. Risk-taking that threatens to violate this social compact by perhaps harming others or disobeying social standards creates moral quandaries.

The moral conundrums surrounding taking risks are complicated and multidimensional, requiring people to negotiate a difficult terrain of ethical considerations, societal obligations, and personal desires. The ability to strike a balance between one's own goals and social responsibilities requires careful consideration of the various outcomes, commitment to moral standards, and awareness of the wider implications of one's activities.

Few ideas spark as much ethical discussion as risk-taking in the context of human decision-making. Risk-taking, from calculating bets to daring expeditions, frequently presents moral quandaries that push us to face the fine line between courage and consequences.

This stimulating subject explores the difficulties people encounter when navigating the perilous waters of uncertainty, delving into the ethical aspects of risk. *This essay tries to examine the moral conundrums raised by taking calculated risks, illuminating the intricate considerations and ramifications involved.*

*Leading ethically while navigating risks with honesty

In the complicated and quickly changing world of today, ethical leadership is essential. Leaders that place a high priority on integrity and manage risks ethically not only foster trust and loyalty among their people but also help their firms achieve long-term success. A framework known as ethical leadership emphasizes how to incorporate moral ideals, beliefs, and behavior into decision-making. Setting the example for moral behavior inside their organizations, ethical leaders serve as role models. They place a high value on sincerity, openness, accountability, and respect for others, fostering an environment of integrity at all levels of the business.

The need for ethical leadership has increased in the connected world of today, where information circulates quickly and public scrutiny is strong. Organizations with moral leaders are more likely to have profitable and sustainable growth. In addition to putting the welfare of their employees first, ethical leaders defend the interests of all parties involved, including clients, shareholders, and the larger community.

An essential difficulty for moral leaders is navigating ethical conundrums. Leaders frequently face situations where they must weigh long-term effects against short-term benefits in an environment of a company that is becoming more complex. It is vital to build a strong ethical compass to direct their conduct because they may be under pressure from stakeholders, have competing interests, and find themselves in unclear situations.

Clear principles, norms, and expectations are defined and communicated by ethical leaders to build a solid ethical basis. This fosters consistency throughout the company and offers a framework for decision-making.

They promote an atmosphere where workers feel comfortable raising ethical questions and voicing their concerns. Leaders can learn important lessons and take proactive steps to address potential hazards by promoting open communication. Ethical leaders provide a good example for their teams by acting following the principles they uphold. They set an example for others by acting with integrity, honesty, and accountability. They make sure that workers are aware of the organization's ethical norms, give them the resources they need to make moral decisions, promote lifelong learning, and set up effective decision-making procedures that take ethical considerations into account. To make wise and moral decisions, they promote critical thinking, ethical reasoning, and the investigation of different viewpoints. They encourage transparency by disclosing decisions, justifications, and potential dangers openly. They promote a culture of accountability and moral behavior by holding both themselves and their teams accountable for their deeds.

Organizations can get many advantages from ethical leadership, such as improved stakeholder interactions, increased employee engagement, and decreased legal and financial risks. Ethical leaders build trust, encourage creativity, and establish a favorable workplace culture that draws top talent by modeling integrity.

To thrive and achieve long-term success, organizations need ethical leadership in a time of increasing dangers and ethical complexities. In a company environment that is always changing, adopting ethical leadership principles is not just a moral requirement but also a competitive advantage.

Chapter 7
Sports and the Pursuit of Glory

*Pushing the Limits in Extreme Sports

Extreme sports have become incredibly popular in recent years, capturing the attention of thrill-seekers and those addicted to adrenaline all around the world. These fearless people take risks by doing things that push their physical and mental limits to the very maximum. Extreme sports are an arena where barriers are broken and fear is vanquished, from mountain biking down precarious paths to cliff diving into merciless waters. The thrilling excitement of the unknown is one of the main reasons why people are drawn to extreme sports. Risk arouses the senses, sending adrenaline rushing through the body and causing a state of acute concentration. Athletes who engage in extreme sports report feeling completely present and in harmony with their bodies. It is a very addicting activity because the powerful surge one feels at these times produces a great sensation of aliveness and release.

Extreme sports demand a high level of mental toughness in addition to their physical demands. Athletes must have constant will, self-control, and bravery to face the risks they will inevitably face. Pushing oneself to the maximum both physically and mentally results in personal development and self-discovery.

Extreme sport participants grow resilient, learn to face their fears, and have a profound grasp of their potential. They are constantly pushing the limits of what is possible because of their relentless pursuit of self-improvement and mastery. Extreme sports have a special sense of accomplishment and joy, but they are also risky. Every action carries a unique mix of hazards, from physical harm to potentially fatal scenarios. Participants in any activity rock climbing, skydiving, or big wave surfing must carefully evaluate and handle any potential risks. To reduce the hazards involved with these sports, rigorous preparation, careful scheduling, and adherence to safety procedures are necessary. However, even taking all possible safeguards, human error and the unpredictable nature of nature cannot be completely eradicated. Athletes who compete in extreme sports are acutely aware of the cost of their passion. They frequently make emotional and physical sacrifices to pursue their objectives. They invest endless hours into developing their abilities, putting up with demanding training schedules, and persevering through pain and setbacks. Athletes understand that there is always a chance of getting hurt and that even one slip-up or bad decision can have far-reaching effects. Nevertheless, despite the difficulties and potential risks, their unrelenting quest for the unusual is motivated by their passion for the activity they have chosen. Extreme sports competitors are always looking to push the envelope, challenging themselves, and redefining what is possible. The boundaries of what is possible in these activities are continually expanding thanks to technological developments and a burgeoning community of like-minded people. World records are broken, new disciplines are created, and risky exploits are completed. These pioneers of extreme sports serve as role models for others, motivating them to leave their comfort zones, follow their passions, and face the uncharted. Extreme sports, where pushing the limits is a way of life, are inherently risky. Extreme sports aficionados have a mindset defined by their quest for adrenaline, personal development, and an unwavering determination to overcome obstacles. Even while there are risks involved with these activities that should never be taken lightly, the benefits of overcoming obstacles, discovering oneself, and experiencing the exhilaration of overcoming fear make the journey worthwhile. Extreme sports competitors are modern-day explorers who defy gravity and social norms to live a life away from the norm.

*Understanding Competitive Psychology

A fascinating field of study that explores the complex ways in which the human mind responds to obstacles and the desire to achieve is the psychology of competition. We are wired for competition, and comprehending its psychological underpinnings can help us understand why some people perform better under pressure than others. A crucial component of competitive endeavors is motivation. The desire to perform better than others, receive praise, or accomplish particular objectives can be a strong motivator. Our innate need for approval is frequently tapped through competition, which can also inspire ambition and tenacity. Some people thrive on the surge of adrenaline that comes from intense competition, using it as a motivator for development and personal growth. They regard challenges as chances rather than hurdles, and they use competition as benchmarks for their development. On the other hand, rivalry can also cause unpleasant feelings and undesirable outcomes. Anxiety and self-doubt might result from a fear of failing or being judged by others. Some people could experience performance anxiety as a result of feeling too much pressure to achieve, which would be detrimental to their talents. Their potential may be hampered by their crippling dread of failing or failing to live up to expectations. For one to keep a healthy competitive mindset, understanding and controlling these negative feelings are essential. The distinction between intrinsic and extrinsic motivation is covered in the psychology of competition.

A desire to excel internally that is motivated by personal fulfillment, delight, or a sincere interest in the activity itself is known as intrinsic motivation. Extrinsic motivation, on the other hand, is brought on by outside forces like incentives, admiration, or rivalry. Although both types of motivation can affect performance, the intrinsic drive is more likely to be enduring and supportive of long-term success. People who are intrinsically motivated are more likely to persevere in the face of difficulties and find meaning in the process rather than only paying attention to the results. The effect of mindset on performance is another component of the psychology of competitiveness. A growth mindset is frequently linked to resilience, persistence, and adaptability because it is defined by the conviction that abilities can be developed through effort and study. People that have a growth mentality welcome challenges, ask for feedback, and consider failures as chances to do better.

A fixed mindset, on the other hand, might result in a fear of failure and aversion to challenges because it assumes that abilities are inherent and immutable. Maintaining a positive and fruitful approach to competition requires cultivating a growth mindset.

The consequences of social comparison and self-evaluation are also covered in the psychology of competitiveness. People frequently assess their success and advancement by comparing themselves to others in competitive circumstances. Social comparison has a double-edged effect since it can spur improvement and serve as a motivator, but it can also breed resentment, jealousy, and unhealthy competitiveness. People must establish a balance between positively exploiting social comparison and avoiding negative consequences on their self-esteem and mental health. *The psychology of competition includes a wide range of elements that affect people's drive, perspective, and performance.* Although it may be a strong driver of development and success, competition also comes with risks and difficulties. Individuals can better manage their motivation, develop a growth mentality, and negotiate the challenging dynamics of competition by being aware of its psychological components.

Chapter 8
Societal Impact of Risk

*Political, medical, and social risks are intertwined.

Risk can appear in many different aspects of a person's life in the complicated and connected world of today. It influences the course of societies and individuals, permeating the fields of politics, medicine, and social movements. We may learn more about risk's complex nature and its significant impact on our lives by exploring these three topics. As the setting for power dynamics and decision-making, navigating the Perils of Power Politics entails taking risks.

To achieve political goals, it is frequently necessary to negotiate a maze of risks, trade-offs, and possible outcomes.

Politicians and policymakers must balance the need for change and stability with the needs of various groups, as well as with socioeconomic difficulties. Politics involves risk not only in the choices taken but also in the results of inaction or poorly thought-out acts.

The high-stakes risks that politicians must take are exemplified by issues like *international conflicts, climate change, economic inequality, and civil rights*. The study of medicine, which aims to maintain and restore health, is not risk-free. Numerous ethical conundrums and difficulties are brought about by the complexity and progress in medical science. Medical personnel must continually evaluate the dangers connected to treatment methods, cutting-edge treatments, and drug side effects. Consideration of the potential risks and rewards is necessary to strike a balance between patient autonomy, beneficence, and non-maleficence.

Allocating resources, prioritizing public health measures, and managing global pandemics are additional challenges faced by healthcare systems and governments. These choices come with enormous hazards that affect people, communities, and society as a whole. Social movements have the potential to bring about transformative change since they are the result of widespread demands for social fairness. Social movements nevertheless face inherent hazards notwithstanding their quest for development. Even if their goals may be good, the techniques used might have unforeseen consequences and cause societal divisions. There is a risk of polarization, unrest, and conflicts between opposing factions while attempting to balance the need for social change with the maintenance of social order. Social movements also have to contend with internal difficulties such as leadership rivalries, ideological disagreements, and vested interest co-optation.

The risk is not just that they won't achieve their objectives, but also that social cohesiveness and political stability may suffer in the long run as a result. Politics, medicine, and social movements are related while having different characteristics, and the hazards they pose overlap.

The availability and caliber of medical services are impacted by political decisions that affect healthcare policy and regulations. Political agendas and policy priorities can be influenced by social movements, which could change public health programs and healthcare systems.

The political environment can also be affected by medical developments and public health emergencies, which can lead to discussions about how to allocate resources, promote equity, and strengthen communal bonds. awareness of the broader implications and managing risks successfully relies on an awareness of these interdependencies.

*Risks from Climate Change Worldwide

One of the world's most important challenges at the moment is climate change.

Globally, ecosystems, economies, and human welfare are all under serious risk due to their extensive consequences. It is critical to comprehend the complex issues posed by climate change and create long-term solutions as temperatures rise, sea levels rise, and extreme weather events become more frequent.

Beyond just rising temperatures, climate change's effects are becoming more severe. We are seeing a world being molded by the forces of a changing climate, from altered precipitation patterns to adjustments in ecosystems. Rising sea levels are a threat to coastal areas and low-lying places as a result of the faster melting of polar ice caps and glaciers. Heatwaves, hurricanes, floods, and droughts are occurring more frequently and are becoming more severe, which disrupts ecosystems, harms infrastructure, and reduces agricultural output.

As species struggle to adapt to rapidly changing conditions, climate change disturbs ecosystems and poses a threat to biodiversity. The stability of ecosystems and the services they offer are significantly impacted by this loss of biodiversity. Climate change affects how diseases are distributed geographically, allowing vector-borne illnesses like malaria and dengue fever to spread to new areas and pose a greater threat to public health.

Existing global dangers are amplified by climate change, and new ones are also created. To handle these risks' cascading impacts, a comprehensive strategy is needed due to their interdependence. *Here are some significant worldwide concerns that have been made worse by climate change.* Global food security is put at risk as a result of altered rainfall patterns and an increase in the frequency of extreme weather events. Additionally, freshwater resources' accessibility and quality are impacted by shifting precipitation patterns. Infrastructure

damage, rising insurance rates, and interruptions in supply chains are just a few of the ways that climate-related catastrophes can cause significant financial losses. In vulnerable groups and underdeveloped nations, the effects are more severe. *Communities are compelled to migrate as a result of rising sea levels, severe weather, and damaged ecosystems, which pose new difficulties for social cohesion, resource access, and global cooperation.*
Conflict risk may increase due to competition over finite resources, such as water and arable land, which

is made worse by climate change. This has consequences for both regional and global security. Unified global action is necessary to address climate change and the hazards it poses. *To mitigate and adapt to a changing world, governments, businesses, communities, and people all have a part to play.* Mitigating climate change requires a shift to renewable energy sources, the adoption of sustainable lifestyles, and a reduction in greenhouse gas emissions.

Global collaboration is facilitated by international agreements like the

Paris Agreement. Communities can adapt to the effects of a changing climate by investing in infrastructure, sustainable agriculture, and disaster preparedness to build resilience to climate change.

To promote behavioral change and create a sense of urgency among people and communities, it is crucial to increase public understanding of climate change and its implications.

Chapter 9
Learning from Failure

*Lessons from Risk Gone Wrong: The Wisdom of Mistakes

In the course of life, errors are frequently perceived as gaffes or failures, which causes regret and disappointment. However, many errors contain a hidden gem, a priceless lesson that may be learned from the experience of taking a risk and having it go wrong. A thorough examination of how failures, setbacks, and mistakes may impact our lives, promote growth, and eventually help us succeed is presented in The Wisdom of Mistakes. This compelling narrative reveals the transforming impact of accepting our mistakes and learning from them via the stories of people who have faced failure head-on. We explore how vulnerability enables us to take risks, stretch our limits, and question the status quo by using personal tales and examples from real life.

We invite growth and self-discovery by embracing vulnerability, which opens up a world of possibilities for us. Failure can be frightening, but this chapter demonstrates that it requires bravery to own up to our errors and grow from them. We highlight people who have faced failure head-on with fortitude and tenacity, illuminating the fact that genuine achievement frequently rises from the ruins of defeat. We can have the guts to take chances and devote ourselves unwaveringly to our passions by accepting failure as a step on the path to achievement.

The value of adaptation is one of the important lessons that may be drawn from the risk that goes wrong.

Through engrossing accounts of people who have experienced setbacks, we see their capacity to adapt, change course, and eventually transform their errors into chances for growth and innovation. A trait called resilience makes it possible for us to recover from failure, setbacks, and errors. Their stories provide potent reminders that our failures do not define us but rather lay the groundwork for our future progress both personally and professionally. The knowledge we get from our blunders transcends the confines of our particular existence. We see the enormous effect that vulnerability and transparency can have on creating resilient communities and cultivating a culture that values the knowledge acquired from a risk gone wrong via touching experiences and motivational tales.

*The Bottom Line: Embracing the Depths of Risk

Finally, accepting the full extent of risk can be a transformational and joyful experience. Even though taking a risk can be fundamentally frightening and unknown, doing so is the only way to fully realize our potential, experience personal growth, and accomplish extraordinary feats. We expose ourselves to the danger of failure as well as the opportunity for enormous success when we leave our comfort zones and travel into unfamiliar territory. Risk forces us to face our anxieties and limitations, pushing us to exceed our expectations and reach new heights. It forces us to use our imaginations, adjust to new circumstances, and strengthen our resilience in the face of difficulty.

Additionally, taking up risks frees us from the restrictions of a life that is unchanging and boring. By accepting the unknown, we widen our horizons and expose ourselves to a world of opportunities. We broaden our perspectives on life, experience new things, and pick up worthwhile lessons. As we come to value the process and the lessons it teaches us, the trip itself gains value on par with the final product. Risk carries the possibility of failure, but it's crucial to understand that failure is not a final destination but rather a stop along the way to success. Every obstacle provides a chance for development and education. By taking on risks, we increase our capacity for resiliency, perseverance, and the capacity to succeed again after failing. These characteristics support our long-term success and enjoyment and are necessary for personal growth.

Taking a chance does not mean behaving carelessly or without deliberation. It involves thoughtfully assessing the benefits and drawbacks of many options before making a decision. It calls for thorough planning, cautious preparation, and a readiness to adjust and change direction as needed. An awareness of one's responsibilities and the potential effects on oneself and others should go along with taking risks. So let's dare to embrace the heights of risk and set out on a quest for self-realization and contentment.

www.ingramcontent.com/pod-product-compliance
Lightning Source LLC
Chambersburg PA
CBHW071512220526
45472CB00003B/996